S.95
LOE370

Copyright © 1986

OSSIAN PUBLICATIONS LTD
World Copyright, Made in Ireland

All rights reserved, including the right of reproduction
in whole or in part in any form or by any means without
the prior permission of the publishers

The publishers wish to thank the National Gallery of Ireland
for permission to reproduce 'The Piping Boy' by Nathaniel Hone

Design, layout and typesetting by John Loesberg
Music origination by Set On Music, Bantry

Printed by Lee Press, Cork, for

OSSIAN PUBLICATIONS LTD
PO Box 84, Cork, Ireland

ISBN 0 946005 31 1

OMB 33

Selecting two hundred tunes out of the vast treasure house of Irish music turned out to be a difficult task. The final selection represents a very personal choice - a mixture really of some pretty well-known items, together with a host of tunes from unusual sources, not readily available in print. The guiding principle in selecting the tunes was not so much based on their traditional 'rooting' but rather on the sheer melodic strength of each tune.

Just like good literature will allow an effective translation into another language, most of the music in this book is musically outstanding and may be played equally on 'traditional' or 'classical' instruments without losing any of its magic.

Irish music, I believe, can hardly be treated as one homogeneous entity - so much of the music comes from entirely different sources, such as the dance tunes, which are nowadays much to the forefront - the old unacconpanied *Sean Nos* singing, a tradition all but extinct - and the curious blend of the harpmusic, with its classical overtones.

Like in most other collections all forms of Irish music are here represented in roughly equal proportions - a reflection of the fact that most musicians will want to try their hand at any Irish piece and most performances will usually include a mix of dance music, ballads, slow airs, Carolan tunes etc.

The bulk of melodies found in the established collections and manuscripts tend to be dance tunes. Tens of thousands of these have been taken down by many collectors such as O'Neill, Pigot, Forde, Bunting and others. A lot of these tunes can be rather straightforward and many may be musically mediocre - they merely outline the musical form that dictates the dance-steps. The same can be said of other types of music : in early European artmusic, very large numbers of courtly dances (the bulk of which were peasant dance tunes originally) such as the galliards, bransles, minuets etc. will often yield only a few musically satisfying examples. Obviously for most dances rhythm was the main ingredient, while only a small proportion of all tunes can be considered as musically interesting.

Of course when a dance is in full swing many musicians achieve extraordinary levels of musical dexterity and will quite often clothe the 'bones' of a basically plain tune with dazzling virtuosity and a perfect sense of improvisation.

Many of the airs included were originally Gaelic songs and this should be borne in mind when playing; an unhurried approach will be found best for most of them, with much scope for the introduction of some ornamentation.

The repeats in the dance tunes are more or less optional: if the player is not accompanying dancers, tunes may be played in any sequence with any amount of repeats in order to make it stand up as an interesting composition in its own right.

If this small collection may form some way of introduction to Irish music - especially to those who normally would not be conversant with any traditional idiom - such as classically trained musicians - I will feel richly rewarded.

For many aspects of the music I was utterly dependent on many professional players, who helped me every step of the way with all manner of advice, with unfailing interest and enthusiasm. I can barely express enough gratitude for the time, care and energy extracted from so many friends, scholars and musical wizards who helped me out in so many ways. Without them I would have tumbled into a 'black hole' of zillions of tunes, never to be retrieved. I'd like to thank especially:

Tomás O Cannain, Matt Cranitch, Mícheál O Súilleabháin, 'Hammy' Hamilton,
The late T.C.Kelly, Albert Bradshaw, Jim Lockhart of RTE, the staff of the Cork City & County Libraries, Ailil Shaughnessy and Mary McLoughlin of the Kevin Street Music Library, Dublin.

John Loesberg

The Comely Girl both Tall and Straight

Air

An Fhaillingín Mhuimhneach
The Little Munster Cloak

Air

Fear an Bhata
The Man with the Stick

Air

Mary Griffen

Air

Peigín Leitir Mhóir
Peggy of Lettermore

Air

The Little Rushlight

Air

The Green Bushes

Air

Give Me Your Hand

Ruari Dall O'Cathan (17th Cent.)

Air

Black-eyed Susan
Air

Airdí Cuan
Air

Eireóidh Mé Amáireach
I will rise tomorrow

Air

The Lark in the Clear Air

Air

Farewell to Spain
Air

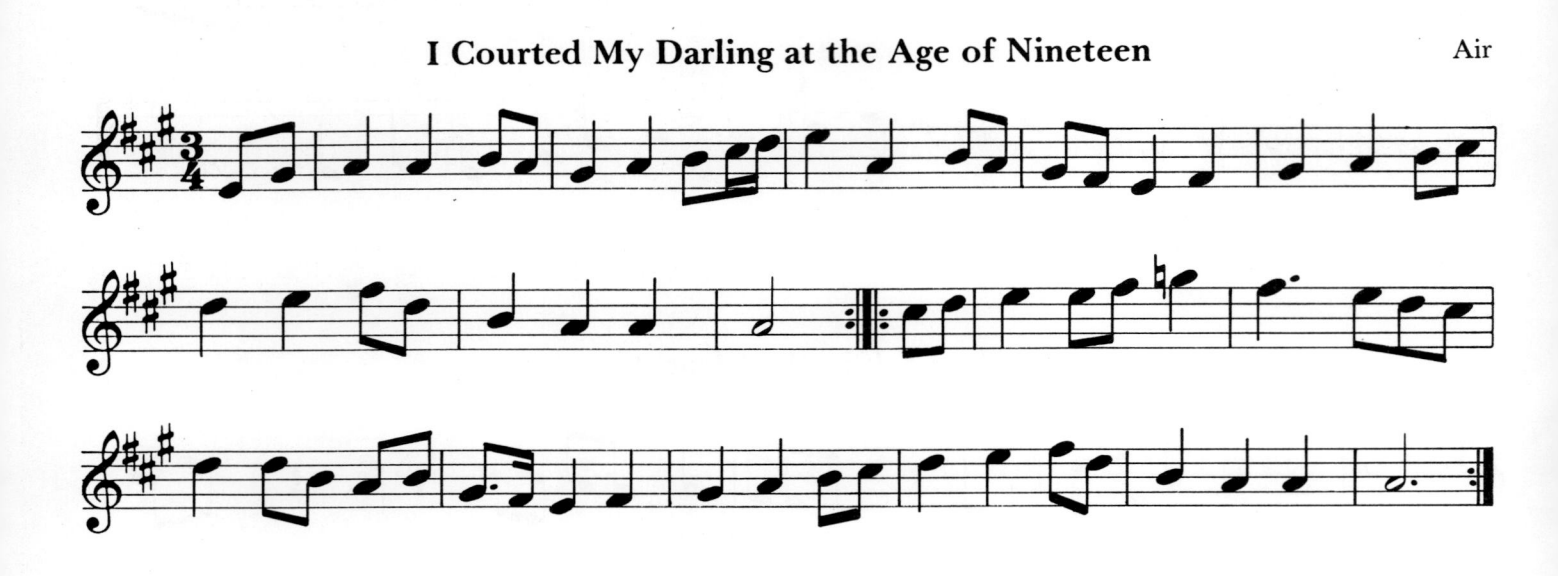

I Courted My Darling at the Age of Nineteen
Air

No Title
Air

Lady Iveagh

Thomas Connallan

The Lambs on the Green Hills

Air

Past One O' Clock

Air

Sally Gardens

Air

Miss Hamilton
Air

Cape Clear
Air

The Parting Glass

Air

The Banks of the Suir

Air

Callino Casturame
Air

An Gcumhain leatsa an Oíche Úd
Do you remember that Night
Air

The Poor Irish Boy
taken down by Handel in 1742

Tom Billy's Jig

King Charles' Jig

No Surrender !

Jig

The Blooming Meadows

Jig

Cunnla

Jig

Old Kilfenora Jig

Belfast Ham
Jig

Morrison's Jig

The Dingle Regatta
Jig

The Cliffs of Moher
Jig

Súiste Buí
The Yellow Flail

Jig

Since Love is the Plan

Jig

Slán agus Beannacht le buairibh a' Tsaoil
Farewell to the Troubles of the World

Jig

Cailín an Túirne
Maid at the Spinning Wheel

Jig

Amhran an Tae
Song of the Tea

Jig

Lillibulero

Jig

The Limerick Tinker
Double Jig

Billy O'Rourke
Double Jig

Kiss the Quaker's Wife

Single Jig

Oíche Nollag
Christmas Eve

Single Jig

The Long Note

Single Jig

The Butterfly
Slip Jig

Fine

DC al Fine

Philip McCue
Slip Jig

Dilín O Deamhas
Sing-Song
Slip Jig

Drops of Brandy

Slip Jig

The Kid on the Mountain

Slip Jig

Wink and She'll Follow You

Slip Jig

Dennis Murphy's Slide

Cúil Aodha Slide

Mary Willie's Slide

The New Line to Macroom

Reel

The Kilfenora Reel

Lady Townsend's Delight

Reel

The Dawn
Reel

Boil the Breakfast Early
Reel

The Pigtown
Reel

Croghan's Reel

The Teetotaller Reel

The Devil to Pay

Reel

Miss Walker's Favourite
Reel

Miss Elizabeth Casey's Fancy
Reel

The Bog-blossom
Reel

O'Flynn's Fancy
Reel

Molly my Darling

Reel

The Derry Hornpipe

A Kerry Hornpipe

The Devil's Dream
Hornpipe

The Showman's Hornpipe

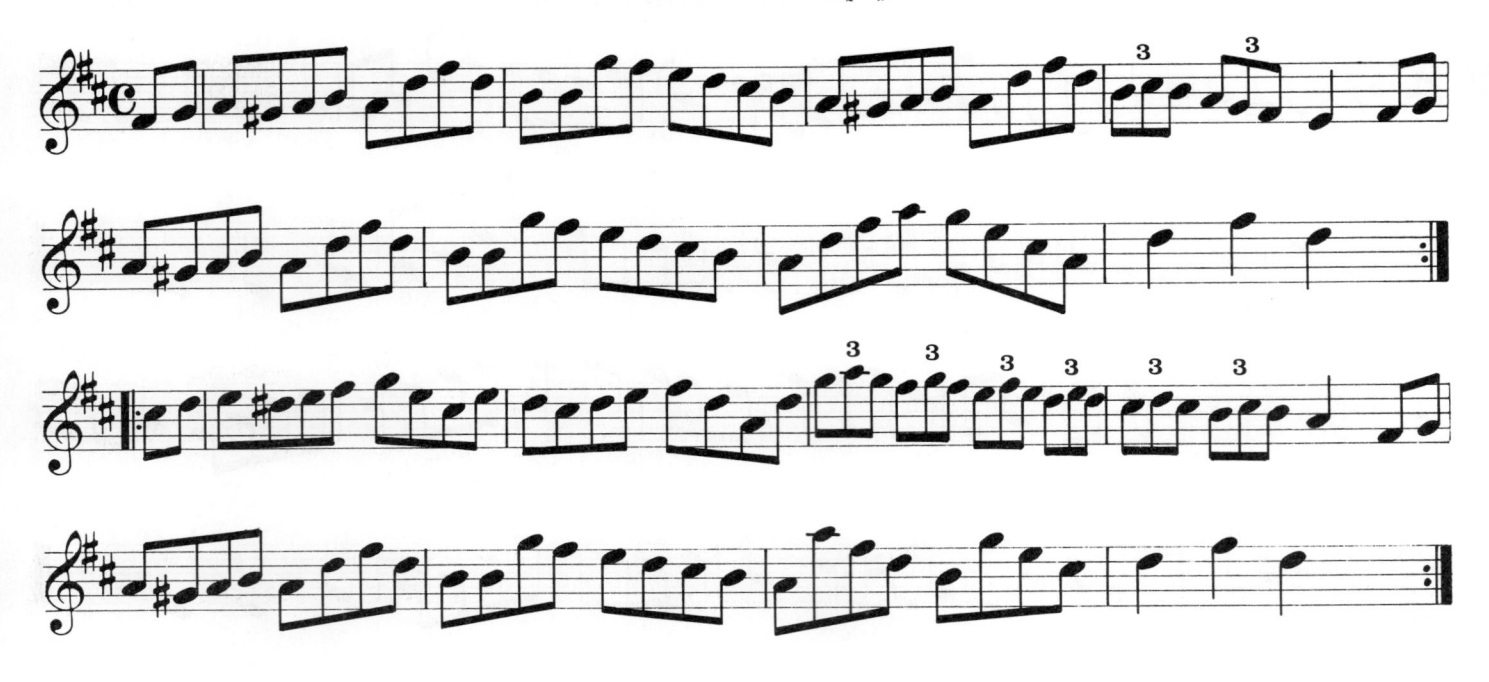

The Pullet
Hornpipe

Whiskey, You're the Devil

Hornpipe

The Harvest Home

Hornpipe

King of the Fairies

Set Dance

The Piper o'er the Meadow Straying

Set Dance

The Ace and Deuce of Pipering

Set Dance

Jockey at the Fair

Set Dance

The Knocknabower Polka

Ballydesmond Polka

The Maids of Ardagh
Polka

Reynard the Fox
March

The Eagle's Whistle

March

A Clan March

O'Neill's Cavalcade

March

Brian Boru's March

More of Cloyne

March

Sir Charles Coote

Carolan

Bridget Cruise

Carolan

Suantraí
Lullaby

Lullaby

Wintergarden Quadrille

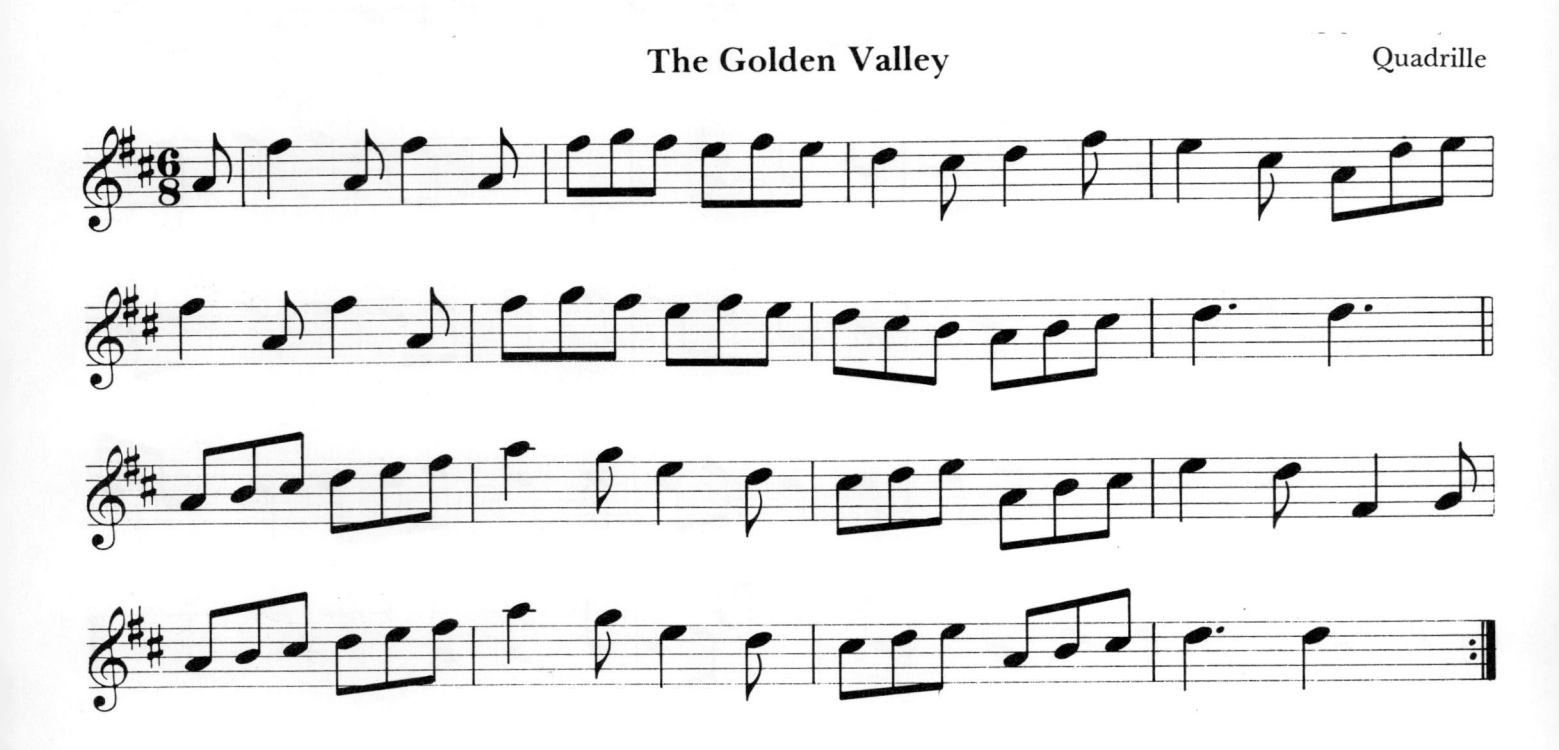

The Golden Valley
Quadrille

Mo Ghrá-sa mo Dhia
My Sweet Lord

Hymn

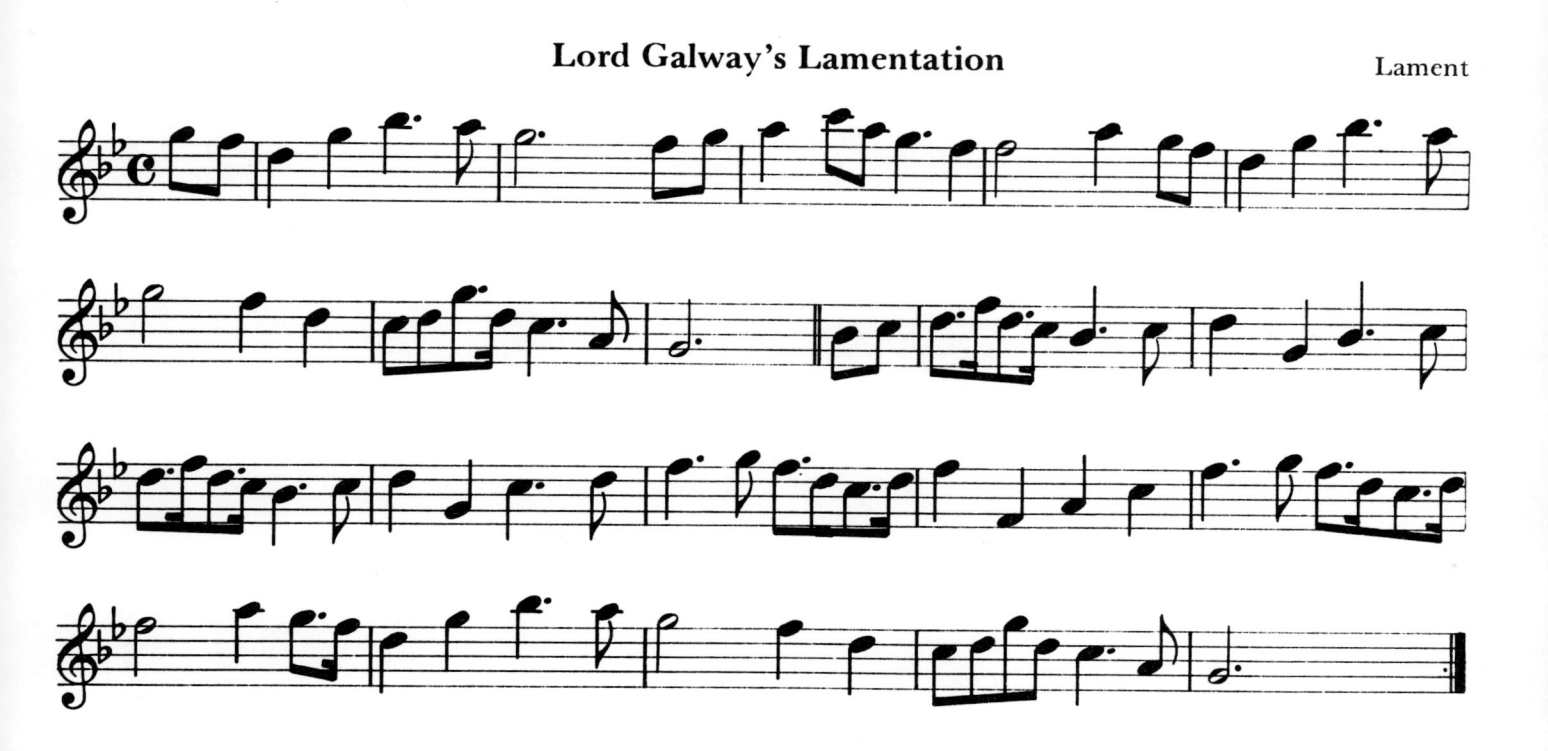

Lord Galway's Lamentation

Lament